Brain and its

Mathematics

Subhajit Ganguly

Tech Reads

Brain and its Mathematics

Subhajit Ganguly

Tech Reads

Science Books

First published in 2014

ISBN-13: 978-1505674910 ISBN-10: 1505674913
http://subhajitgangulyauthor.wordpress.com

email: gangulysubhajit63@gmail.com

Contents

Chaotic Fuzziness

References

ACKNOWLEDGMENTS

This book is a culmination of the good wishes of many individuals, without whom nothing would have been possible. I take this opportunity to thank them all from the bottom of my heart. Hope my endeavor does justice to all the good wishes and aspirations surrounding it.

Complex Fuzzy Abstraction: The Brain Logic

Key Ideas:

Taking abstraction as the starting point, we build a complex, *self-organizing fuzzy logic system*. Such a system, being built on top of abstraction as the base, turns out to be just a special outcome of the laws of abstraction. As the system is self-organizing, it runs automatically towards optimization. Using such a system in neural networks, we may come as close as possible to the workings of the human brain. The *abstract fuzzy optimization* is seen to follow a Gaussian distribution.

Introduction:

There are quite a large number of differences between the way present day computers work and the way the brain works. The very way in which basic processing is done by computers varies vastly from the way the brain processes information. Computers, working on binary logic, can take into account only *high* or *low* states. They can have a number of inputs that are processed by a single processing unit. After being processed, the input(s) can have a single output or a number of outputs. On the other hand, brain cells seem to be able to process information using abstract fuzzy logic that leads to more energy optimization. In fact, estimates suggest that present day computers use up ten million times more energy to process the same amount of information that the human brain does.

This does not take into account, however, the accuracy and speed of decision making by the two systems for large enough data inputs. The basic difference between the today's computers and the brain lie in the fact that while computers have only two logical states, the brain uses can have many such states and in-between states simultaneously generating patterns similar to attractor maps. Decisions are asymptotic functions of such maps in the case of the brain, while in computers the decisions are only approximate points in the output space. As such, all waypoints in the input system itself can act as decision making units inside the brain. The way in which this happens is no longer linear (as in computers), but nonlinear. This nonlinear information processing by the brain is vastly superior to the linear processing used by computers in arriving at decisions.

Abstraction lies at the heart of the complex, self-organizing fuzzy logic that is used by the brain. In fact, this logic is the direct fallout and a special case of abstraction. The *Theory of Abstraction* and the principle of *Zero Postulation* describes directivity towards optimized solutions and cluster formation in the decision making space as inherent properties of the system itself. They must also be able to describe the formation of various structures and patterns in the decisions that the system can arrive at. As such, it is of great interest for us to investigate how these structures are formed in the decision space. A theory that is able to describe the world in totality has to keep the number of basic postulates it depends upon to zero or near zero.

Reductionism hits a dead end in this regard. On the other hand, abstraction as the starting point of building up a theory may be seen to be of fitting use. It would be much more than a new way of tackling the problem. Even abstract postulates do away with the shackles that bind our theories into the system and bar them from being total descriptions of the system. The abstraction we are talking about here may be defined as, "Postulation of non-postulation" or, in other words, "A system of postulation that gives equal weights to all possible solutions inside the system and favors none of such solutions over others."

Abstraction automatically gives rise to optimized solutions within the universal set of all possible solutions, as has been shown in this book. It is these optimized solutions that make up and drive the non-abstract parts of the world, while the non-optimized solutions remain 'hidden' from the material world, inside the abstract world. Zero postulation or abstraction as the basis of theory synthesis allows us to explore even imaginary and chaotic non-favored solutions as possibilities. With no postulation as the fundamental basis, we are thus able to pile up postulated results or favored results, but not the other way round. We keep describing such implications of abstraction in this book. We deal with the abstraction of observable parameters involved in a given system and formulate a similar basis of understanding them.

Let us consider the example of a three-point isolated system. Let the points be 'A', 'B' and 'C'. Let A and B be decision points, whereas, C be situated anywhere on the straight line joining A and B. The decision flow of both A and B tends to move in all possible directions. These possible directions include the directions towards each other. Thus, at point C, for obvious reasons, an additional effect will be felt due to the tendency of decision to flow from A to B and from B to A, as compared to all other directions.

The points A, B and C being considered parts of an isolated system and all three points being assumed fundamentally similar (with the only difference that A and B contain decisions, while C is empty), the factors R and S must be equal. Thus, we have:

$$\frac{F}{T} = c\frac{\lambda}{D}$$

D being considered the *decision distance* between A and C and x the distance between A and B (say), the *decision distance* between B and C is $D - x$. This *decision distance* can be any length of any given dimensions (as determined by the scaling-ratio of observations, the simplest of dimensions being two) between two points in the decision space.

The effect on C due to the decision-point A can thus be written as,

$$\frac{F_A}{T_A} = \text{ }\text{\'E}\frac{\lambda_A}{x}$$

Similarly, the effect on the empty point C due to the decision-point B is,

$$\frac{F_B}{T_B} = c\,\frac{\lambda_B}{D - x};$$

where F_A and F_B are the respective values of flows towards the point C due to A and B, respectively. T_A and T_B are the respective values of time and λ_A and λ_B are the respective values of the differences in concentrations of decisions between A and B.

Substituting x in the above two equations, we have,

$$c\,\frac{T_A \lambda_A}{F_A}$$

$$= D - c\,\frac{T_B \lambda_B}{F_B} \qquad \ldots (1)$$

Considering the points to be having equal factors, i.e., considering $\lambda_A = \lambda_B = \lambda$ (say), $F_A = F_B = F$ (say) and $T_A = T_B = T$ (say), equation (1) reduces to,

$$c\frac{T\lambda}{F} = D - c\frac{T\lambda}{F}$$

i.e.,

$$\frac{F}{T} = 2c\left(\frac{\lambda}{D}\right) \qquad \dots (2)$$

Equation (2) describes fundamentally the effect (i.e., the flow F in time T) of two decision-points having same factorial conditions regarding one or a number of already existing decisions.

Pattern Generation:

Considering a collection of such points and applying a statistical approach, the logistic equation for $\left(\dfrac{F}{T}\right)$ can be written as,

$$
2c\left(\frac{\lambda}{D}\right)_{t+1}
$$

$$
= 2Kc\left(\frac{\lambda}{D}\right)_{t}\left[1\right.
$$

$$
\left. - 2c\left(\frac{\lambda}{D}\right)_{t}\right]
$$

i.e.,

$$\left(\frac{\lambda}{D}\right)_{t+1}$$

$$= K \left(\frac{\lambda}{D}\right)_{t} \left[1 - 2c \left(\frac{\lambda}{D}\right)_{t}\right] \quad \dots (3)$$

where K is a constant.

Also, the quadratic map can be written as,

$$2c \left(\frac{\lambda}{D}\right)_{t+1} = K - \left(2c \frac{\lambda}{D}\right)_{t}^{2}$$

i.e.,

$$2c \left(\frac{\lambda}{D}\right)_{t+1}$$

$$= K - 4c^2 \left(\frac{\lambda}{D}\right)_{t}^{2} \quad \dots (4)$$

All trajectories described by the quadratic map become asymptotic to $-\infty$ for

$$K < -0.25 \text{ and } K > 2$$

As we deal with the flow of a given decision towards one given point or the effects on a given point, the expression for the attractor for each such point can be written as,

$$\left(2c\frac{\lambda}{D}\right)^* = \left(1 - \frac{1}{K}\right) \qquad ...(5);$$

where $0 < K < B$.

$\left(2c\frac{\lambda}{D}\right)^*$ is a point in the desired dimensional plot into which the trajectories seem to crowd. As we do not need to deal with more than one attractor or periodic point, the trajectories will tend to revisit only the attractor point concerned, to the desired level of accuracy of observations and calculations.

For $K \geq 3$, the trajectory behaviour becomes increasingly sensitive to the value of K. There are a few more points to be noted regarding the dependence of the trajectory behavior on the values of K:

1.   For $K \leq 1$, the attractor is a fixed point and has a value Ψ.

2.   For $1 < K < 3$, the attractor is a fixed point and its value is > 0 but < 0.667.

3.   For $3 \leq K \leq 3.57$, period doubling occurs, with the attractor consisting of

$2, 4, 8,$ etc., periodic points as K increases within that range.

4.   For $3.57 < K \leq 4$, we have the region of chaos, where the attractor can be erratic (chaotic with infinitely many points) or stable.

For all calculations, the desired conditions may be placed at the attractor. A trajectory never gets completely and exactly all the way into an attractor though, but only approaches it asymptotically. In the region of chaos, we apply the method of searching for windows or zones of K-values for which iterations from any initial conditions will produce the periodic attractor, instead of a chaotic one. For the logistic equation(3), the most common such zone lies at $K \approx 3.83$ and for the quadratic map(4), at $K \approx 1.76$.

Let us consider a given representation with fractal dimension D_F. The fractal dimension is purely geometrical, i.e., it only depends on the shape of the representation. A suitable probability measure $d\mu$, according to the particular phenomenon considered is assigned to the given representation. A coarse grained probability density, as the decision of the hypercube Λ_i of size l is defined as,

$$P_i(l) = \int_{\Lambda_i} d\mu(x)$$

where $i = 1,2,3, \dots, N(l)$.

The information dimension D_I is such that,

$$\sum_{i=1}^{N(l)} P_i \ln(P_i)$$

$$\simeq D_I \ln(l) \qquad \qquad ...(6);$$

where $D_I \leq D_F$.

The number of boxes containing the dominant contributions to the total decision and thus relevant part of the information, is,

$$N_R(l) \propto l^{-D_I} \qquad \qquad ...(7).$$

For each box Λ_i, $D_I = D_F$ for a uniform distribution. When $D_I < D_F$, the measure itself may be called fractal since it is singular with respect to the uniform distribution,

$$P^* = \frac{1}{N(l)} \propto l^{D_F}$$

For each box Λ_i. Thus, $\dfrac{P_i}{P_i^*}$ can diverge in the

limit of vanishing l.

Simulations of the decision-information scaling yields,

$$\langle P_i(l)^q \rangle \equiv \sum_{i=1}^{N(l)} P_i(l)^{q+1}$$

$$\propto l^{q \cdot d_q + 1} \qquad \qquad \dots (8).$$

The d_q are the Renyi dimensions which generalize the information dimension $D_I = d_1$ as well as the fractal dimension $D_F = d_0$. If the d_q's are not constant, anomalous scaling is to be employed and, as the order q varies, the amount of the difference $D_q - D_F$ gives a first rough measure of the heterogeneity of the probability distribution.

The moment generic observables A computed on scale l is such that,

$$\langle A(l)^q \rangle \propto l^{g(q)} \qquad \ldots (9)$$

Anomalous scaling, i.e., a non-linear shape of the function $g(q)$ is the more common situation, where one does not require unnecessarily to consider only a finite number of scaling components. In some cases, one may observe strong time variations in the degree of chaoticity. This intermittency phenomenon involves an anomalous scaling with respect to time-dilations identifying the parameter e^{-t}

with the parameter l used in spatial dialations of the decision space. A measure of the degree of intermittency requires the introduction of infinite sets of exponents which are analogous to the Renyi dimensions and can be related to a multifractal structure given by the dynamical system in the functional trajectory space.

The Grassberger-Procaccia correlation dimension ν is defined by considering the scaling of the correlation integral,

$$C(l) = \lim_{M \to \infty} \frac{1}{M^2} \sum_i \sum_{j \neq i} \theta \left(l - \left| x_i - x_j \right| \right);$$

where θ is the Heaviside step function and $C(l)$ is the percentage of pairs (x_i, x_j) with distance $|x_i - x_j| \leq l$.

In the limit $l \to 0$,

$$C(l) \propto l^v.$$

In general,

$$v \leq D_F.$$

v is a more relevant scaling index than D_F since it is related to the point probability distribution on the attractor, while D_F cannot take into account an eventual homogeneity in the visit frequencies.

Let us define the number of points in an F-dimensional spherical representation of the decision space, with radius l and centre at x_i as,

$$n_i(l) = \lim_{M \to \infty} \frac{1}{M-1} \sum_{j \neq i} \theta \, (l$$
$$- \, |x_i$$
$$- \, x_j|) \qquad \dots (10).$$

We must introduce a whole set of generalized scaling exponents

$$\langle n(l)^q \rangle$$
$$= \lim_{M \to \infty} \frac{1}{M} \sum_{i=1}^{M} n_i(l)^q$$
$$\propto l^{\emptyset(q)}$$

where $\emptyset(1) = \nu$.

Considering a uniform partition of decision space into boxes of size l it is convenient to introduce the probability $P_K(l)$ that a point x_i falls into the Kth box. In this case, the moments of P_K can be estimated by summing up the boxes,

$$\langle p(l)^q \rangle = \sum_{K=1}^{N(l)} P_K(l)^{q+1}$$

$$\propto l^{q \cdot d_{q+1}} \qquad \ldots (11)$$

A moment of reflection shows:

$$\emptyset(q)/q = d_{q+1}$$

because of the ergodicity $n_i(l) \sim P_K(l)$, if x_i belongs to the Kth box and since one can use either an 'ensemble' average (weighted sum over the boxes) or a 'temporal' average (sum of the time evolution $x(l)$).

The fractal dimension for $q = -1$ is,

$$D_F = d_0$$

$$= -\emptyset(-1)$$

while the correlation dimension is,

$$\nu = d_2$$

$$= \emptyset(1)$$

According to the Theory of Physical Abstraction, each point x should have the same singularity structure,

$$\Delta V_x(r) \propto r^h, h$$

$$= \frac{1}{3} \qquad \qquad ...(12)$$

In other words $\varepsilon(x)$ tends to be smoothly distributed in a region of R^3. The eddy turn-over time and the error deviation per unit decision at scale r are defined as,

$$t(r) \sim \frac{r}{\Delta V(r)} \qquad \qquad ...(13)$$

and

$$E(r) \sim \Delta V(r)^2 \qquad \qquad ...(14)$$

The transfer rate of error deviation per unit decision from the eddy at scale r to smaller eddies is then given by

$$\tilde{\varepsilon}(r)$$

$$= \frac{E(r)}{t(r)} \sim \frac{\Delta V(r)^3}{r} \qquad \text{...} (15)$$

Since,

$$\varepsilon_x(r) = \left(\frac{1}{r^3}\right) \int\limits_{\Lambda_x(r)} \varepsilon(y)d^3y,$$

$[\Lambda_x(r)$ is a cube of edge r around x we have,

$$\int\limits_{\Lambda_x(r)} \varepsilon(y)d^3y \sim r^3 \qquad \text{...} (16)$$

$r \to 0$ means r in the initial range and the regions containing a large part of $\varepsilon(x)$ are a physical approximation of a fractal structure. In this β −model approach,

$$\int_{\Lambda_x(r)} \varepsilon(y)d^3y \propto \begin{cases} r^{D_F} & if\ x \in S \\ 0 & if\ x \notin S \end{cases}$$

in an equivalent way

$$\Delta V_x(r) \propto \begin{cases} r^h & if\ x \in S \\ 0 & if\ x \notin S; \end{cases}$$

where $h = (D_F - 2)/3$

At scale r, there is only a fraction,

$$r^{3-D_F} \propto \frac{r^{-D_F}}{r^{-3}}$$

occupied by active eddies.

The transfer error deviation from the eddy at scale l_n (active eddy) to the scale l_{n+1} is

$$\varepsilon_n \propto \frac{v_n^3}{l_n}.$$

Since, the error deviation transfer rate is constant in the cascade process, for $\beta = 2^{D_F - 3}$, we have,

$$\varepsilon_n = \beta \, \varepsilon_{n+1}, \frac{v_n^3}{l_n}$$

$$= \beta \, \frac{v_{n+1}^3}{l_{n+1}} \qquad \qquad \dots (17)$$

Iterating, we have,

$$v_n$$

$$\propto l_n^{1/3} (l_n/l_0)^{\frac{D_F - 3}{3}}$$

Each eddy at scale l_n is divided into eddies of scale l_{n+1} in such a way that the energy transfer for a fraction β of eddies increases by a factor $\dfrac{1}{\beta}$, while it becomes zero for the other

ones.

In order to generalize the β-model, we have at scale l_n, N_n active eddies. Each eddy $l_n(k)$ generates active eddies covering a fraction of volume $\widetilde{}_{n+1}(k)$. k labels the mother-eddy and $k = 1, ..., N_n$.

Since the rate of energy transfer is constant among mother-eddies and their effects, we have,

$$\dfrac{v_n(k)^3}{l_n}$$

$$= \beta_{n+1}(k)\dfrac{v_{n+1}(k)^3}{l_{n+1}} \qquad \text{... (18)}$$

The iteration of v_n gives an eddy generated by a particular history of fragmentations $[\beta_1, \ldots, \beta_n]$, such that,

$$v_n \propto l_n^{1/3} \left(\prod_{i=1}^{n} \beta_i \right)^{-1/3} \qquad \ldots (19)$$

The fraction of volume occupied by an eddy generated by $[\beta_1, \ldots, \beta_n]$ is $\prod_{i=1}^{n} \beta_i$, such that,

$$\langle |\Delta V(l_n)|^P \rangle \propto l_n^{P/3} \int \prod_{i=1}^{n} d\beta_i \; \beta_i^{(1-P/3)} P(\beta_1, \ldots, \beta_n)$$

With no correlation among different steps of the fragmentation, i.e., with $P(\beta_1, \ldots, \beta_n) = \prod_{i=1}^{n} P(\beta_i)$, the exponent concerned,

$$\zeta_P$$

$$= \frac{P}{3}$$

$$- \ln_2\left\{\beta^{(1-P/3)}\right\} \qquad \ldots (20)$$

For a given transport of decision, between an initial and a final point, let the trajectory of the initial point $x_0 = x(0)$ be denoted by,

$$x(t) = f^t(x_0)$$

Expanding $f^t(x_0 + \delta x_0)$ to linear order, the evolution of the distance to a neighbouring trajectory $x_i(t) + \delta x_i(t)$ is given by the

Jacobian   matrix J,

$$\delta x_i(t) = \sum_{j=1}^{d} J^t(x_0)_{ij} \ \delta x_{oj},$$

$$J^t(x_0)_{ij}$$

$$= \frac{\delta x_i(t)}{\delta x_{oj}} \qquad \ldots (21)$$

A trajectory of a decision as moving on a flat surface, as is the simplest decision space (it being a plane), is specified by two position coordinates and the direction of motion. The Jacobian matrix describes the deformation of an infinitesimal neighborhood of $x(t)$ along the transport. Its eigenvectors and eigenvalues give the directions and the corresponding rates of expansion or contraction. The trajectories that start out in an infinitesimal neighborhood separate along the unstable directions (those whose eigenvalues are greater than unity in magnitude), approach each other along the stable directions (those whose eigenvalues are less than unity in magnitude), and maintain their distance along the marginal directions (those whose eigenvalues equal unity in magnitude).

Holding the hyperbolicity assumption (i.e., for large n the prefactors a_i, reflecting the overall size of the system, are overwhelmed by the exponential growth of the unstable eigenvalues Λ_i, and may thus be neglected), to be justified, we may replace the magnitude of the area of the ith strip $|B_i|$ by $\dfrac{1}{|\Lambda_i|}$ and consider the sum,

$$\lceil n = \sum_i^n \frac{1}{|\Lambda_i|};$$

where the sum goes over all periodic points of period n. We now define a generating function for sums over all periodic orbits of all lengths,

$$\lceil z$$

$$= \sum_{n=1}^\infty \lceil n \, z^n \qquad \ldots (22)$$

For large n, the nth level sum tends to the limit $\lceil n \to e^{-n\gamma}$, so the escape rate γ is determined by the smallest $z = e^\gamma$ for which equation (22) diverges,

$$\lceil z \approx \sum_{n=1}^{\infty} (ze^{-\gamma})^n$$

$$= \frac{ze^{-\gamma}}{1 - ze^{-\gamma}} \qquad \ldots (23)$$

Making an analogy to the Riemann zeta-function, for periodic orbit cycles,

$$\lceil z = -z\frac{d}{dx}\sum_{p} \ln(1 - t_p);$$

$\lceil(z)$ is a logarithmic derivative of the infinite product

$$\frac{1}{\zeta(z)} = \prod_{p}(1 - t_p), t_p$$

$$= \frac{z^{n_p}}{|\Lambda_p|} \qquad \ldots (24)$$

This represents the dynamical zeta function for the escape rate of the trajectories of decision-transport.

Abstraction says that points inside the decision space cluster to form *decision directions* of a given property, at the desired scaling-ratio. Let us consider one such system of decision making, inside which its constituent points have the tendency to form clusters.

Prediction:

In such transactions, the family of evolution-maps f^t form a group. The evolution rule f^t is a family of mappings of strips of transport B, that we may consider, such that,

1) $f^0(x) = x$

2) $f^t[f^{t'}(x)] = f^{t+t'}(x)$

3) $(x, t) \rightarrow f^t(x)$ from $B \times R$ into

B is continuous;

where t represents a time interval and

$t \in R.$

For infinitesimal times, we may write the trajectory of a given transaction as,

$$x(t + \tau) = f^{t+\tau}(x_0)$$

$$=$$

$$f[f(x_0, t), \tau] \quad \ldots (25)$$

The time derivative of this trajectory at point

$x(t)$ is,

$$\frac{d}{d\tau}\dot{\ }\bigg|_{\tau=0} = \partial_\tau f[f(x_0,t),\tau]|_{\tau=0}$$

$$= \dot{x}(t) \qquad \dots (26)$$

The vector field is a generalized velocity field,

$$\dot{x}(t)$$

$$= v(x)$$

If x_q represents an equilibrium point, the trajectory remains stuck at x_q forever. Otherwise, the trajectory passing through x_0 at time $t = 0$ may be obtained by,

$$x(t) = f^t(x_0)$$

$$= x_0 + \int_0^t d\tau \, v[x(\tau)], x(0)$$

$$= x_0 \qquad\qquad\qquad ...(27)$$

The Euler integrator, which advances the trajectory by $\delta\tau \times \text{velocity}$ at each time step is,

$$x_i = x_i + v_i(x)\delta\tau.$$

This may be used to integrate the equations of the dynamics concerned.

In our decision/perception plane a fuzzy set L_F may be defined as:

$$L_F: L \to [0,1], \qquad\qquad ...(28).$$

where L is a domain of elements (universe of discourse).

For every particular value of a variable $L_i \in L$ the degree of membership to fuzzy set L_F is $L_F(L_i)$.

Equation (28) describes how we can incorporate a fuzzy complex number or FCN in our decision/perception plane.

L_F in the universe of discourse L is defined by the complex membership grade function $\mu L_F(L_i)$. The complex membership grade function or CMG is defined as:

$$\mu L_F(L_i) = L_F(L_i)e^{ic}$$

$$\ldots(29).$$

The Cartesian representation of CMG for $\mu L_F(L_i) = \mu L_F(c_i + ir_i)$ is:

$$\mu(c_i, r_i) = \mu(c_i) + ir_i$$

$$\ldots(30)$$

And, the polar representation is:

$$c_i e^{isr} \qquad \ldots(31),$$

the scaling factor S being in the interval $(0, 2\pi]$.

The degree of fulfillment or DOF of any given proposition follows CMG and lies in the interval [0,1].

According to the definition of transformation of coordinates:

$$\mu(c_i, r_i) \Leftrightarrow c_i e^{isr}$$

The operators Λ and V defining t-norm and s-norm respectively and L_i being the set of fuzzy numbers concerned, the fuzzy set of a function of L_i has the membership function:

$$\mu(c_i', r_i') =$$
$$V_{c_i'=f(L_i)}[\mu(c_1, r_1) \wedge \mu(c_2, r_2) \wedge \mu(c_3, r_3) \ldots \wedge \mu($$

Using Lyapunov exponents for the measure L,

and replacing $2c \left(\dfrac{\lambda}{D} \right)$ by a quantity $'\tau'$, we

have:

$$\frac{d}{d\tau} f^n (L) = \frac{\delta n}{\delta o}$$

i.e.,

$$\frac{\delta n}{\delta o} = \prod_{i=1}^{n} f'(L_i)$$

...(32).

$$b = \frac{1}{n} \log_e \left(\frac{\delta n}{\delta o} \right)$$

i.e.,

$$b = \frac{1}{n} \sum_{i=1}^{n-1} \log_e |f'(L_i)|$$

...(33).

where b is a constant (the local slope of all possible measures), and

$$\Psi = \lim_{n \to \infty} \frac{1}{n} \sum_{i=0}^{n-1} \log_e |f'(L_i)|$$

...(34).

where Ψ is a constant.

Distribution:

Signal processing time in *abstract fuzzy optimization* seems to follow a Gaussian curve.

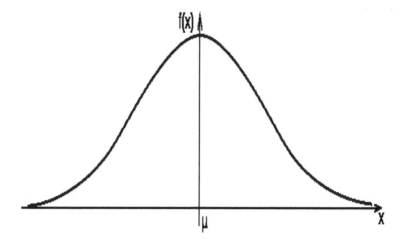

Fig. 1: A Gaussian Curve.

For such a curve, if the height of the peak is R,

the mean is μ and the standard deviation σ,

then,

$$f(C, \mu, \sigma) = \frac{1}{\sigma\sqrt{2\pi}} e^{-\frac{(x-\mu)^2}{2\sigma^2}}$$

$$= \frac{1}{\sigma\sqrt{2\pi}} e^{-\frac{C^2}{2\sigma^2}}$$

μ being taken to be zero in the super-complex
plane of decision making.

For the simplest case of a two dimensional decision plane,

$$L_i = \frac{1}{2\pi\sigma^2} e^{-\frac{(C^2+R^2)}{2\sigma^2}} \qquad \ldots (35).$$

A two-dimensional elliptical Gaussian function for such a case, may be expressed as:

$$f(C, R)$$
$$= L_i e^{-a(C-C_0)^2 + 2b(C-C_0)(R-R_0) + c(R-R_0)^2}$$

where a, b and c forms a positive definite matrix as:

$$\begin{bmatrix} a & b \\ b & c \end{bmatrix}$$

A measure for precision in any given direction of decision making is given by the covariance matrix,

$$V = \frac{\sigma^2}{\sqrt{2}P_C P^2} \begin{bmatrix} \dfrac{3}{2c} & 0 & \dfrac{-1}{a} \\ 0 & \dfrac{2c}{a^2} & 0 \\ \dfrac{-1}{a} & 0 & \dfrac{2c}{a^2} \end{bmatrix}$$

Where, the precision of the system is represented by P.

Depending upon the value of precision involved, the number of activated states follows a sigmoid distribution:

$$n(t) = \frac{1}{1 + e^{-t}}$$

Conclusion:

Natural processes, including decision making follows non-linear pathways that give rise to emergence phenomena. Patterns arise in the whole that cannot be wholly attributed to the sum of the parts. The whole decision making process is way more than the sum of the individual processes involved. From the *Theory of Abstraction*, we know how *information energy* changes with changes in the scaling ratio. The same can be observed in the decision making process too. The difference in dissipation energy information (and as such deviation in a given direction of decision making), which tends to infinity as the number of constituent points inside it tends to infinity. In this respect, at large enough scaling-ratios, the universe seems to work in a similar way as the brain does.

Building a Foolproof Navigation System:

Fuzzy Logic Emulating the Brain

Key Ideas:

Our aim is to help build a machine that can reduce the possibility of mishaps in navigation to zero. For that devise a new system of numbers, in which the real numbers are represented on the y-axis and complex numbers on the x-axis. Inside such a system, we incorporate the equivalent Ideal Fuzzy

Logic that can be used by the machine to predict and avoid mishaps.

Introduction:

Natural processes are vastly emergent phenomena and each new result is always the source of new emergence. To cope with nonlinear control problems, binary logic is no longer sufficient. What we need is an ideal Fuzzy Logic that not only can process complex numbers with utmost efficiency, but also 'thinks' in terms of complex numbers. Such a system also needs to be as simple as possible for us and for machines to work with.

A perfectly efficient navigation system will be able to receive inputs that have all sets of possible values. These values may be real or imaginary. Such a system will be particularly efficient in dealing with imaginary numbers and will be able to reduce the probability of a mishap to zero.

The Fuzzy logic that we have today is yet to incorporate imaginary numbers with the desired level of satisfaction, and many serious problems remain in this.

We develop a new system of numbers that can make use of the equivalent Fuzzy Logic inside it. A machine that runs on such a system will be able to predict and avert mishaps completely.

Let us consider a system of numbers, where all complex numbers are real and all real numbers are complex, i.e.,

$R \Leftrightarrow C$

...(1),

R and C being real numbers and complex numbers, respectively.

In such a system, all individual positive numbers are negative and all individual negative numbers are positive, for complex numbers, while all original real numbers are multiplied by i.

Thus,

$C=x+iy \Rightarrow C'=-x+\sqrt{1}(-y) = -(x \pm y) \in R$

...(2.1)

And

$R \Rightarrow R'=-iR =-(0+iR) \in C$

...(2.2).

Thus, in such a system, we have two lines of numbers:

1. The set of originally complex numbers, transformed into real ones, represented on the x-axis.

2. The set of originally real numbers, transformed into complex ones, represented on the y- axis.

The original system transforms, therefore, into two separate and mutually perpendicular number lines, with individual numbers being points on the corresponding lines.

An Ideal Navigation System:

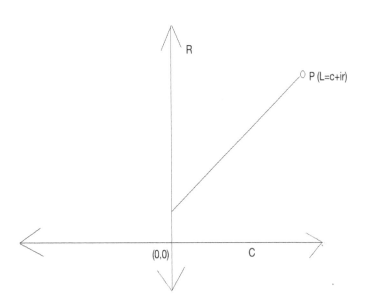

Fig. 1: A simple illustration of signal-processing by a machine running on the new system.

Fig. 1 shows a simple illustration of signal processing by a machine. The set of complex numbers on the x-axis and the set of real numbers on the y-axis give rise to the parameter L for any given point P in the super-imaginary complex plane of decision making. The parameter L represents both the real and the imaginary parts of the signal and incorporates them into the abstract decision making/perception plane.

In the complex decision/perception plane:

$L = c + ir$

...(3).

c and r being the complex and real coordinates for the point P.

The basic difference between *classical sets* and *fuzzy sets* is that while classical sets allow only a dual degree of membership, a fuzzy set can incorporate any real value between the dual states concerned. A characteristic membership function assigns 0 to an element that is not a member of a given classical set, while it assigns a value of 1 to an element that is a member of that set. The degree of membership to a fuzzy set can take any value in the real unit interval [0, 1].

In our decision/perception plane a fuzzy set L_F may be defined as:

$L_F: L \rightarrow [0,1]$,

...(4).

where L is a domain of elements (universe of discourse).

For every particular value of a variable $L_i \in L$ the degree of membership to fuzzy set L_F is L_F (L_i).

Equation (4) describes how we can incorporate a fuzzy complex number or FCN in our decision/perception plane.

L_F in the universe of discourse L is defined by the complex membership grade function $\mu L_F(L_i)$. The complex membership grade function or CMG is defined as:

$$\mu L_F(L_i)= \qquad\qquad L_F(L_i)e^{ic}$$

...(5).

The Cartesian representation of CMG for $\mu L_F(L_i)= \mu L_F(c_i+ir_i)$ is:

$$\mu(c_i, r_i)= \mu(c_i)+ir_i$$

...(6)

And, the polar representation is:

$$c_i e^{isr}$$

...(7),

the scaling factor s being in the interval $(0, 2\pi]$.

The degree of fulfillment or DOF of any given proposition follows CMG and lies in the interval $[0,1]$.

According to the definition of transformation of coordinates:

$$\mu(c_i, r_i) \Leftrightarrow c_i e^{isr}$$

The operators $\wedge$ and $\vee$ defining t-norm and s-norm respectively and L_i being the set of fuzzy numbers concerned, the fuzzy set of a function of L_i has the membership function:

$$\mu(c_i', r_i') =$$
$$V_{c_i'=f(L_i)}[\mu(c_1, r_1) \wedge \mu(c_2, r_2) \wedge \mu(c_3, r_3) \ldots \wedge \mu(c_n, r_n)]$$
...(8).

Operators and Functions in the New Logic:

OR:

The maximum s-norm (smax) may be used to calculate the DOF concerned. P and Q being two possible values under consideration,

$$DOF(L = P + Q) =$$
$$smax[DOF(P), DOF(Q)] =$$
$$max[DOF(P), DOF(Q)] \quad ...(9).$$

Truth Table

P	Q	max(L)=max(P,Q)
0	0	0
0	1	1
1	0	1
1	1	1

AND:

The minimum t-norm (tmin) may be used to calculate the DOF concerned. P and Q being two Possible values under consideration,

DOF(L= $P \cdot Q$)=

$tmin[DOF(P), DOF(Q)] =$

$min[DOF(P), DOF(Q)]$ ...(10).

Truth Table

P	Q	min(L)=min(P,Q)

0	0	0
0	1	0
1	0	0
1	1	1

NOT:

The complement or negation is used to calculate the DOF concerned. $\bar{L}$ being the complement of L,

$$DOF(\bar{L}) \qquad = \qquad 1\text{-}DOF(L)$$

...(11).

Truth Table

L	$\bar{L}$
0	1

1	0

De Morgan's Operations:

De Morgan's Involution holds as:

$$\neg(P \wedge Q) = \neg P \vee \neg Q$$

and

$$\neg\neg L = L$$

...(12).

where $\neg$ is the NOT operator.

Also, De Morgan's laws hold as:

$$NOT(P \text{ AND } Q) \Leftrightarrow (NOT\ P) \text{ OR } (NOT\ Q)$$

And

$$NOT\ (P \text{ OR } Q) \Leftrightarrow (NOT\ P) \text{ AND } (NOT\ Q)$$

...(13).

Now, the relations (13) also translate to:

$$1 - \min[DOF(P), DOF(Q)] \Leftrightarrow \max[1$$
$$- DOF(P), 1 - DOF(Q)]$$

And

$$1 - \max[DOF(P), DOF(Q)] \Leftrightarrow \min[1 -$$
$$DOFP, 1 - DOFQ \quad ...(14).$$

Chaotic Fuzziness:

In order to incorporate chaotic instances, the ideal Fuzzy Logic may start with a basic starting measure as the standard reference, from which it will calculate the required differences with respect to other values. It may even take one attractor as its reference. However, the manners of functionality of the fuzzy operations that both will follow will be just the same.

For a given transport of parameterization of the degree of membership between an initial and a final point in consideration, let the trajectory of the initial point of reference $L_o = L(o)$ be denoted by,

$$L(t) = f^t(L_o)$$

Expanding $f^t(L_o + \delta L_o)$ to linear order, the evolution of the distance to a neighbouring trajectory $L_i(t) + \delta L_i(t)$ is given by the Jacobian matrix J,

$$\delta L_i(t) = \sum_{j=1}^{d} J^t(L_o)_{ij} \; \delta L_{oj},$$

$$J^t(L_o)_{ij} = \frac{\delta L_i(t)}{\delta L_{oj}}$$

...(15).

A trajectory of the shift in degree of
membership as moving on the
decision/perception plane is specified by two
position coordinates and the direction of
motion. The Jacobian matrix describes the
deformation of an infinitesimal neighbourhood
of $L(t)$ along the shift.

Holding the hyperbolicity assumption (i.e., for
large n the prefactors a_i, reflecting the overall
size of the system, are overwhelmed by the
exponential growth of the unstable eigenvalues
Λ_i, and may thus be neglected), to be justified,
we may replace the magnitude of the area of
the ith strip $|B_i|$ by $\frac{1}{|\Lambda_i|}$ and consider the sum,

$$\lceil n = \sum_{i}^{n} \frac{1}{|\Lambda_i|};$$

Where the sum goes over all periodic points of period n. We now define a generating function for sums over all periodic orbits of all lengths,

$$\lceil z = \sum_{n=1}^{\infty} \lceil n \, z^n$$

...(16).

For large n, the nth level sum tends to the limit $\lceil n \to e^{-n\gamma}$, so the escape rate γ is determined by the smallest $z = e^{\gamma}$ for which $\lceil z$ diverges,

$$\lceil z \approx \sum_{n=1}^{\infty} (ze^{-\gamma})^n = \frac{ze^{-\gamma}}{1-ze^{-\gamma}}$$

...(17).

Making an analogy to the Riemann zeta-function, for periodic orbit cycles,

$$\lceil z = -z \frac{d}{dx} \sum_p \ln(1 - t_p);$$

$\lceil(z)$ is a logarithmic derivative of the infinite product

$$\frac{1}{\zeta(z)} = \prod_p (1 - t_p), t_p = \frac{z^{n_p}}{|\Lambda_p|}$$

This represents the dynamical zeta function for the escape rate of the trajectories of quantum-transport. The fraction of initial x whose trajectories remain within B at time t may decay exponentially,

$$[t = \frac{\int_s dx\, dy\, \delta[y - f^t(x)]}{\int_s dx} \rightarrow e^{-\gamma t}$$

...(18).

Considering a collection of such points and applying a statistical approach, the logistic equation (due to May, 1967) for L can be written as,

$$L_{t+1} = KL_t[1 - L_t]$$

...(19).

where K is a constant.

Also, the quadratic map (due to Lorentz, 1987) can be written as:

$$L_{t+1} = K - (L)_t^2$$

...(20).

All trajectories described by the quadratic map become asymptotic to $-\infty$ for $K < -0.25$ and $K > 2$.

As we deal with the flow of a given measure towards a given reference, the expression for the attractor for each such point can be written as,

$$L^* = \left(1 - \frac{1}{K}\right)$$

...(21).

where $0 < K < 4$.

L^* is a point in the desired dimensional plot into which the trajectories seem to crowd. As we do not need to deal with more than one attractor or periodic point, the trajectories will tend to revisit only the attractor point concerned, to the desired level of accuracy of observations and calculations.

In equation (21), for $K \geq 3$, the trajectory behaviour becomes increasingly sensitive to the value of K. There are a few more points to be noted regarding the dependence of the trajectory behaviour on the values of K:

5. For $K \leq 1$, the attractor is a fixed point and has a value 0.

6. For $1 < K < 3$, the attractor is a fixed point and its value is > 0 but < 0.667.

7. For $3 \leq K \leq 3.57$, period doubling occurs, with the attractor consisting of $2, 4, 8$, etc., periodic points as K increases within that range.

8. For $3.57 < K \leq 4$, we have the region of chaos, where the attractor can be erratic (chaotic with infinitely many points) or stable.

For all calculations, the desired conditions may be placed at the attractor. A trajectory never gets completely and exactly all the way into an attractor though, but only approaches it asymptotically. In the region of chaos, we apply the method of searching for windows or zones of K-values for which iterations from any initial conditions will produce the periodic attractor, instead of a chaotic one. For the logistic equation, the most common such zone lies at $K \approx 3.83$ and for the quadratic map, at $K \approx 1.76$.

Using Lyapunov exponents for the measure L,

and replacing $2c\left(\frac{\lambda}{D}\right)$ by a quantity $'\tau'$, we have:

$$\frac{d}{d\tau}f^{n}(L) = \frac{\delta n}{\delta o}$$

i.e.,

$$\frac{\delta n}{\delta o} = \prod_{i=1}^{n} f'(L_i)$$

...(22).

$$b = \frac{1}{n}\log_e\left(\frac{\delta n}{\delta o}\right)$$

i.e.,

$$b = \frac{1}{n}\sum_{i=1}^{n-1}\log_e|f'(L_i)|$$

...(23).

where b is a constant (the local slope of all

possible measures), and

$$\Psi = \lim_{n \to \infty} \frac{1}{n} \sum_{i=0}^{n-1} \log_e |f'(L_i)|$$

...(24).

where Ψ is a constant.

Let $L_t = c_t + ir_t$ and $L_{t+1} = c_{t+1} + ir_{t+1}$ be corresponding FCN measures with complex membership grade function or CMG as $\mu L_F(L_t)$ and $\mu L_F(L_{t+1})$, respectively. We may then perform the basic arithmetic operations as:

Addition:

$$L_t + L_{t+1} = (c_t + c_{t+1}) + i(r_t + r_{t+1})$$

The corresponding membership function is:

$$\mu L_F(L_t + L_{t+1}) \quad =$$

$$V_{L_t+L_{t+1}}[\mu L_F(L_t) \wedge \mu L_F(L_{t+1})]$$

Subtraction:

$$L_t - L_{t+1} = (c_t - c_{t+1}) + i(r_t - r_{t+1})$$

The corresponding membership function is:

$$\mu L_F(L_t - L_{t+1}) =$$

$$V_{L_t-L_{t+1}}[\mu L_F(L_t) \wedge \mu L_F(L_{t+1})]$$

Normalization of L_i:

Considering n number of measures, we have the normalized measure for L_i as:

$$Nor(L_i) = \frac{L_i - \min (L_i)}{\max (L_i) - \min (L_i)}$$

...(25).

$D(P,Q)$ being the distance measure between two normalized fuzzy sets P and Q, within the measure L_i, the degree of match between them is denoted by:

$$M(P,Q) = 1 - D(P,Q)$$

If, $p \in P$ and $q \in Q$, then the maximum distance between the nearest points in P and Q is the Hausdorff distance between P and Q:

$$H(P,Q) = max_{p \in P}[\min_{q \in Q} D(P,Q)]$$
$$= max[\sup_{p \in P} \inf_{q \in Q} D(P,Q), \sup_{q \in Q} \inf_{p \in P} D(P,Q)]$$

where sup represents the supremum and inf the infimum.

IF-THEN relations may be evaluated using corresponding DOFs. As such relations are of fundamental importance in any logical construct, they are of interest to us here. We may use a weighted scaling measure S to get the DOF of the final result of a given IF-THEN relation. For this, we break the IF-THEN relation into its constituent parts i.e., the condition part (IF) and the result part (THEN). As the IF relation is always of the form *constituent 1 AND constituent 2*, we may write the condition DOF as:

$$DOF_{Condition} = \min[DOF(Constituent\ 1), DOF(Constituent\ 2)]$$

The product of the scaling measure S and $DOF_{Condition}$ gives the final result as:

$$DOF_{Result} = S(DOF_{Condition})$$
...(26).

The scaling measure S may be taken as the corresponding Hausdorff distance between the constituents.

Read other books by Subhajit Ganguly. To know more, visit his page here:
http://www.amazon.com/Subhajit-Ganguly/e/B0083SW05E

Or here:

http://subhajitgangulyauthor.wordpress.com

References

1.   A.   Connes,   Trace   formula   in noncommutative geometry and the zeros of

the Riemann zeta function, Selecta Math. (NS) 5 (1999), 29–106.

2.   J.B. Conrey, More than two fifths of the zeros of the Riemann zeta

function are on the critical line, J. reine angew. Math. 399 (1989), 1–26.

3.   P.   Deligne,   La   Conjecture   deWeil   I, Publications Math. IHES 43 (1974),

273–308.

4.   P. Deligne, La Conjecture de Weil II, Publications Math. IHES 52

(1980), 137–252.

5.   Browder, Felix, ed. Mathematical Developments Arising from Hilbert Problems.

American Mathematical Society, 1976.

6.   Kantor, Jean-Michel. "Hilbert's Problems and Their Sequel", Mathematical

Intelligencer 18 (1996): 21 – 30.

7.   Smale, Stephen. "Mathematical Problems for the Next Century", Mathematical

Intelligencer 20 (1998): 7 – 15.

8.   Pier, Jean-Paul, ed. The Development of Mathematics, 1950 – 2000. Birkhauser,

2000.

9. Arnol'd, Vladimir, Michael Atiyah, Peter Lax, Barry Mazur, eds. Mathematics

Tomorrow. International Mathematical Union, 2000.

10. C. Deninger, Some analogies between number theory and dynamical

systems on foliated spaces, Proc. Int. Congress Math. Berlin 1998, Vol. I, 163–186.

11. H.M. Edwards, Riemann's Zeta Function, Academic Press, New York -

London 1974.

12. S. Haran, Index theory, potential theory, and the Riemann hypothesis,

L-functions and Arithmetic, Durham 1990, LMS Lecture Notes 153 (1991), 257–

270.

13. G.H. Hardy, Divergent Series, Oxford Univ. Press 1949, Ch. II, 23–26.

14. H. Iwaniec and P. Sarnak, Perspectives on the Analytic Theory of

L-Functions, to appear in proceedings of the conference Visions 2000, Tel Aviv.

15. A. Iviˇc , The Riemann Zeta-Function - The Theory of the Riemann Zeta-

Function with Applications, John Wiley & Sons Inc., New York - Chichester -

Brisbane - Toronto - Singapore 1985.

16.   N.M. Katz and P. Sarnak, Random matrices, Frobenius eigenvalues

and monodromy, Amer. Math. Soc. Coll. Publ. 49, Amer. Math. Soc., Providence

RI 1999.

17. E. Landau, Primzahlen, Zwei Bd., IInd ed., with an Appendix by Dr.

Paul T. Bateman, Chelsea, New York 1953.

18.   N. Levinson, More than one-third of the zeros of the Riemann zetafunction

are on $\sigma = 1/2$, Adv. Math. 13 (1974), 383–436.

19. J. van de Lune, J.J. te Riele and D.T. Winter, On the zeros of

the Riemann zeta function in the critical strip, IV, Math. of Comp. 46 (1986),

667–681.

20.   H.L. Montgomery, Distribution of the Zeros of the Riemann Zeta Function,

Proceedings Int. Cong. Math. Vancouver 1974, Vol. I, 379–381.

21.   A.M. Odlyzko, Supercomputers and the Riemann zeta function, Supercomputing

89:    Supercomputing   Structures   & Computations, Proc. 4-th Intern.

Conf. on Supercomputing, L.P. Kartashev and S.I. Kartashev (eds.), International

Supercomputing Institute 1989, 348–352.

22.   B. Riemann, Ueber die Anzahl der Primzahlen unter einer gegebenen

Gr¨osse, Monat. der K¨onigl. Preuss. Akad. der Wissen. zu Berlin aus der Jahre

1859 (1860), 671–680; also, Gesammelte math. Werke und wissensch. Nachlass, 2.

Aufl. 1892, 145–155.

23.   Z. Rudnick and P. Sarnak, Zeros of principal L-functions and random

matrix theory, Duke Math. J. 82 (1996), 269–322.

24.   A. Selberg, On the zeros of the zeta-function of Riemann, Der Kong.

Norske Vidensk. Selsk. Forhand. 15 (1942), 59–62; also, Collected Papers, Springer-

Verlag, Berlin - Heidelberg - New York 1989, Vol. I, 156–159.

25. F. Severi, Sulla totalit`a delle curve algebriche tracciate sopra una superficie

algebrica, Math. Annalen 62 (1906), 194–225.

26. C.L. Siegel, ¨Uber Riemanns Nachlaß zur analytischen Zahlentheorie,

Quellen und Studien zur Geschichte der Mathematik, Astronomie und Physik 2

(1932), 45–80; also Gesammelte Abhandlungen, Springer-Verlag, Berlin - Heidelberg

- New York 1966, Bd. I, 275–310.

27. E.C. Titchmarsh, The Theory of the Riemann Zeta Function, 2nd ed.

revised by R.D. Heath-Brown, Oxford Univ. Press 1986.

28. R. Taylor and A. Wiles, Ring theoretic properties of certain Hecke

algebras, Annals of Math. 141 (1995), 553–572.

29. A. Weil, OEuvres Scientifiques–Collected Papers, corrected 2nd printing,

Springer-Verlag, New York - Berlin 1980, Vol. I, 280-298.

30. A. Weil, Sur les Courbes Alg´ebriques et les Vari´et´es qui s´en d´eduisent,

Hermann & Cie , Paris 1948.

31. A. Weil, Sur les "formules explicites" de la th´eorie des nombres premiers,

Meddelanden Fr°an Lunds Univ. Mat. Sem. (dedi´e `a M. Riesz), (1952), 252-

265; also, OEuvres Scientifiques–Collected Papers, corrected 2nd printing, Springer-

Verlag, New York - Berlin 1980, Vol. II, 48–61.

32. A. Wiles, Modular elliptic curves and Fermat's Last Theorem, Annals

of Math. 141 (1995), 443–551.

33. Ganguly, Subhajit (2012): Distribution of Prime Numbers,twin Primes and Goldbach Conjecture.   figshare.
http://dx.doi.org/10.6084/m9.figshare.91653

34. Dave Carr, Jeff Shearer, Nonlinear Control and Decision Making Using Fuzzy Logic in Logix.

35. D.E. Tamir, A. Kandel, Axiomatic Theory of Complex Fuzzy Logic and Complex Fuzzy Classes, Int. J. of Computers, Communications

& Control, ISSN 1841-9836, E-ISSN 1841-9844 Vol. VI (2011), No. 3 (September), pp. 562-576.

36. Li Renjun, Yuan Shaoquiang, Li Baowen, Fu Weihai, Fuzzy Complex Number.

37. Xin Fu, Qiang Shen, Fuzzy Complex Numbers and their Application for Classifiers Performance Evaluation.

38. Ramot, D., Milo, R., Friedman, M., Kandel, A., Complex fuzzy sets. IEEE Transactions on Fuzzy Systems 2002, 10(2): p. 171-186.

38. Ramot, D., Friedman, M., Langholz, G., Kandel, A., Complex fuzzy logic. IEEE Transactions on Fuzzy Systems, 2003, 11(4): p. 450-461

39. Ganguly, Subhajit (2014): Building a Foolproof Navigation System: Fuzzy Logic Emulating the Brain. figshare.

http://dx.doi.org/10.6084/m9.figshare.1093898

40. Arthur, J.V.; Boahen, K. "Recurrently connected silicon neurons with active dendrites for one-shot learning", *Neural Networks, 2004. Proceedings. 2004 IEEE International Joint Conference on,* On page(s): 1699 - 1704 vol.3 Volume: 3, 25-29 July 2004

ABOUT THE AUTHOR

Subhajit Ganguly is a physicist whose areas of expertise include the Theory of Abstraction. His contribution to the theory is noteworthy, to say the least. The other areas of science that he has made notable contributions to include astronomy, mathematics and the Chaos Theory. Zero-postulation is a new concept he has introduced to the theorizing process in

sciences. He is an Advisor to the Figshare
Open Science Platform and is an Ambassador
for the Open Knowledge Foundation.

www.ingramcontent.com/pod-product-compliance
Lightning Source LLC
Chambersburg PA
CBHW051208050326
40689CB00008B/1239